Laughter Lives Here

EVELYN KLIEWER

396
BROADMAN PRESS
Nashville, Tennessee

© Copyright 1982 ● BROADMAN PRESS.
All rights reserved.
4252-03
ISBN: 0-8054-5203-6

Scriptures marked TLB are taken from *The Living Bible*. Copyright ©
Tyndale House Publishers, Wheaton, Illinois, 1971. Used by permission.

Dewey Decimal Classification: 818
Subject Heading: FAMILY LIFE—ANECDOTES, FACETIAE, SATIRE, ETC.
Library of Congress Catalog Card Number: 81-70476
Printed in the United States of America

To mothers, God bless them

Introduction

"Mom," our number one daughter asked recently, "Why don't you write a book about our neurotic family?"

"Wendy," I replied, "that sounds like a winner. What a unique way to let men and women the world over know that with Jesus all things are possible, even survival in a household such as ours!"

Thus this not-so-very-profound book was born. I have followed my philosophy, "A merry heart doeth good like a medicine" (Prov. 17:23), in its writing.

Over the years, I've learned that God blesses those who don't take themselves too seriously. Please indulge yourself in a little laughter, and perhaps shed a few tears, as you share a collection of our family's tales with me.

.

CONTENTS

1
Cow Town

Wendy had been away at college for nearly three years when she decided to bring some of her more sophisticated classmates home for a weekend.

One friend, Brian, inquired, "Is Brawley one of those little cowpoke towns out in the middle of nowhere?"

"That's right," Wendy replied, her blues eyes shining.

"Oh, goody," Brian responded. "I've never been to one of those."

So Wendy issued the formal invitations:

> You, yes you, are invited to a fabulous weekend at the Kliewer Hilton in Brawley, California, March 9-11. A $3 fee will include all meals and round-trip transportation. This is your once-in-a-lifetime opportunity to view the wild west. RSVP.

I was to provide the meals, Wendy the transportation—covered by the three dollars per person. It sounded like a good deal to six adventurous, starving college students, and they all accepted.

The group caught some of Brawley's unique flavor as they drove into town and got tied up in a steer jam. They sat in the car and watched as the herd passed on the highway, kicking up the dust. Choking, Brian asked, "How did your folks ever end up in a place like this?"

Wendy said, "We'll be home soon. I'm sure Mom will be happy to tell you her love story."

After we ate our dinner of Carne Asada (a type of marinated steak native to our valley), refried beans, and tortillas, we sat around in the family room, and I explained how I had managed to get myself from the big city of San Francisco to the tiny town of Brawley.

Kermit, a lonely private stationed at Fort Ord near Monterey, had decided one Thanksgiving to visit his Aunt Marianna in San Francisco. "Can you arrange a date for me?" he asked her. "Nothing serious."

Marianna belonged to the same social club as my mother and asked her if I might be available to show Kermit around the city.

"What does he look like?" I inquired.

"I understand from Marianna that he is tall and slim," Mother replied.

He sounded suitable, so I agreed to the date. When I first eyed him, though, I gasped. Marianna had failed to mention his balding head.

12

On our first date we rode a cable car to Fisherman's Wharf and munched on apples as we walked along the piers, looking at boats and visiting. Kermit shared his after-army plans to teach agriculture and to farm on the side. "That's interesting," I commented, not expecting ever to be involved in that type of life and not really understanding what it was all about.

Much to my surprise, Kermit asked me for another date . . . and another. Auntie and Mother were delighted as they watched our love blossom. And it all happened in the city.

When I answered yes to Kermit's marriage proposal, I had no idea what I was getting into. Yet, I should have been suspicious when his army buddies brought us one hundred pounds of steer manure as a wedding gift!

The first year of marriage, spent on California's Monterey Peninsula, included lolling on the beach at Carmel and numerous rides on the famed seventeen-mile drive which winds along the coast between Monterey and Carmel. Life seemed serene. Then Kermit's army stint ended, and he was interviewed for teaching jobs in Southern California. He came home one Sunday night and announced, "I've signed a contract in Brawley."

"Where's that?" I asked.

"On the desert, down near Mexico. You'll love it."

A faded memory suddenly became vivid. I'd whizzed through Brawley several years earlier on a summer trip. I'd asked myself at that time, noting the infinitesimal size of the town, the heat, and the crickets lining the gutters, *Who would ever live in a place like this*? Now I knew.

The trip to the little yellow stucco house Kermit had chosen for us was, as anticipated, long and hot. We stopped every few miles to water an overheated radiator and to wipe the sweat from our brows. Finally we arrived.

Noting a tomato field across the street from the house and army caterpillars crawling about (those are the kind which travel in units), I sensed I was not cut out to be a farmer's wife. But now that I was one, there seemed little I could do about it.

I did share a measure, a small one to be sure, of Kermit's excitement about starting a new career, even though I wished he had chosen a more populous locale.

My enthusiasm waned as the summer progressed. I longed for fog, for shopping centers, for the theater, for Mother.

How was I to know that my days were soon to be so filled with sheep, swine, and other assorted animals, earthquakes, and handicapped kids that I would have little time for nostalgia?

But I did find ample opportunity for prayer. And many of my conversations with our Lord

14

were desperate: "Oh, God, how can I make it through another day?"

The Lord would reply, "Chin up, kiddo. With me along, you'll survive." And so far, although it sometimes amazes me, I have.

2
Mercy, Lord, There's a Lamb on My Couch!

The other morning I was busy vacuuming the red print carpeting in our large family room when I happened to glance out the back window.

A yellow school bus had pulled up to our back gate and stopped. I watched as Kermit and thirty teenagers piled out, then gathered again in the furthermost corner of our 150-foot lot.

Amid the baas of several lambs, I heard Kermit's voice booming out, "These are the clippers; this is the wool sacker. Now watch closely as I demonstrate how to shear a lamb."

What on earth is going on? I wondered. Suddenly, I realized that Kermit's agriculture class was on a field trip to, of all places, *our* backyard!

Sheep have played an integral role in our lives since moving to Brawley twenty-two years ago. Soon after that first fall semester began, Kermit came home one afternoon and said, "I'm so happy we have a large backyard."

"Really? Why's that?" I questioned, hoping he was about to share plans for a flower garden or perhaps a fish pond.

"It's just perfect for keeping sheep." He explained it was hard to find lambs for his Future Farmers of America students, which they needed for the winter fair, and he was going to experiment with a breeding project.

"Don't sheep smell?" I asked. "Draw flies?"

"No problem. I'll build a pen in the back corner of our lot, and the sheep won't bother you a bit." He pulled out plans for his sheepherder's camp.

From the front, our house looks much like the other houses in our tract. It is individualized by a widened cement driveway, a carport, an assortment of pickup trucks, cars, bicycles, and a planter box of philodendrons.

Now the backyard is unique. The patio sports a blocking stand for grooming lambs, buckets, brushes, clippers, a sheep card, and a full wool sacker. The back right-hand corner of our lot is further devoted to the sheep and other necessary equipment, including, just to name a few items, broken scales, a broken-down pen, another wool sacker, shears, and bales of hay.

Over the years I have had some rather adventurous experiences involving sheep. I vividly recall one incident when a lamb zipped into my house as I opened the door to go outside to hang wash.

The lamb raced straight for the bathroom and refused to budge. This presented quite a problem for me since I was a not-so-agile eight months pregnant. I grabbed a broom and gave chase. The lamb romped playfully about the house, finally jumping on my new living-room couch. "If I ever get my hands on you," I screamed, "I'll turn you into lamb chops." As if to let me know he could read my mind, every time I came near the critter he baaed loudly and gave me an icy stare. Kermit finally came to the rescue after I phoned him at a neighbor's house.

The sheep have proved spunky on numerous occasions, especially during the holidays. The most notable escapade occurred about 5 AM one Christmas when the sheep decided to explore Brawley.

We woke up to a knock at our front door. "Those your sheep running down West D Street?" a policeman asked.

"I suppose so," Kermit answered. "My wife and I'll go round 'em up." I was a not-so-graceful seven months pregnant that time. After several exhausting hours, we herded the sheep back into their pen.

The sheep have not only run interference with my pregnancies but with nearly every family event, including childbirth. In fact it still

18

amazes me that our kids didn't baa when the doctor slapped them on the rear in the delivery room.

Kermit was out collecting sheep when Wendy announced her impending arrival. He made it home just in time to whisk me to the hospital, leaving the sheep bleating in the truck.

Bonnie appeared during our local county fair, and again Kermit drove me to the hospital in his pickup—which was loaded with sheep. The lambs serenaded Bonnie's birth.

Kermit was at the fairgrounds tending sheep when Bruce was born. Kermit was on an out of town trip buying sheep when Scott emerged.

Aunt Evelyn came to help me with Scott. Like I had once been, she was "citified" through and through.

We made a bed for her in our family room. Because it was hot, she opened the back door for air. All went well until about 4 AM when a lamb came to the screen and bleated, wanting in. The animal woke Auntie from a sound sleep, and she let out a blood-curdling scream. We raced to the family room, wondering what new catastrophe had occurred in our household.

As the days progressed Auntie calmed down and, in fact, grew rather fond of the lambs, venturing outdoors occasionally to pet them.

The sheep have, unfortunately or fortunately, depending on whether you speak to Kermit or me, trampled the next-door-neighbor's flowers. This caused us to be recipients of a letter from the city animal-control officer requesting that Kermit find another home for his flock.

Our backyard still looks like something *Better Homes and Gardens* would feature in their humor section. And it took a lot of praying before I learned to live with sheep in it.

My prayers would go something like this: "Lord, you know how I feel about sheep and flies. I'm tired of wading through sheep droppings when I hang out the wash. Any suggestions?"

God spoke very quietly inside of me. "Evelyn, the Bible is full of analogies about sheep and shepherds. Aren't you pleased that I have arranged for you to make firsthand observations to aid your understanding of this relationship?"

Never before had I thought of Kermit's project in that light. A fascinating study began for me. Through a combination of backyard observation, supplementary reading in a sheep manual, and Bible study, I learned plenty—such as the fact that sheep need scads of tender, loving care from their shepherd. After my study I even managed to hop around the droppings without complaint.

Eventually—God bless the animal control

officer—Kermit gave up his breeding project. Even so, our yard remains the delivery stable when Kermit buys sheep for his students and has continued to be the local shearing shop.

Excuse me, I hear a knock at our front door. "Oh, hi, Debbie. That's sure a cute lamb you have there. Just take him around back and tie him to the fence. Mr. Kliewer will be with you in a moment."

3
Let's Not Carry
Visual Aids Too Far

Bees have an affinity for Kermit. One time he was helping a beekeeper and was stung by a swarm. On another occasion, he was fishing in nearby Salton Sea when a bee flew to the boat, stung him, and quickly departed.

Once, he had the window of his pickup truck open and, as he drove, a bee flew in the window, stung him, and flew away.

Since Kermit is allergic to bees, he swells from the stings and ends up needing medical attention. Why he decided to teach a bee unit at the high school, I'll never know.

It was early in his career. He moved a colony of bees into his agriculture classroom as part of a unit study. The front of the display was glass. On the back side, he ran a pipe through a hole and vented it to the outside through a cooler.

Some of his more exuberant students immediately plugged the hole with a paper cup. Kermit worked to free the bees, finally succeeding by opening a louvered window, reaching through the top, and pulling out the cup.

Bees flew all over the room. Kermit was the first to leave, followed by his thirty students.

The bees also swarmed around campus. Lydia Gonzales, a plump little Spanish teacher, was innocently walking down a path, heading toward the school office.

All of a sudden, the bees took after her. She ran as fast as her short legs would carry her, straight to the principal.

"Help!" she screamed at Mr. Edney.

Mr. Edney had an inkling as to the origin of the bees. He found Kermit and cornered him. "Kliewer, do you know anything about bees on campus?"

"Yes, sir," Kermit replied politely. "I have sixty thousand of them flying around."

"Round them up," the principal ordered. "And do it fast."

In the process of collecting the bees, Kermit got stung on his thumb. It swelled up like a pear. He headed for the doctor's office and his usual medication.

My husband has decided it is safer to teach units on sheep and hogs. And that's what he's been doing ever since he was accused of carrying visual aids too far.

24

4
Vacations I'd Rather Forget

You'd think Webster of dictionary fame never had any children, even though he did. Strange that he could define a vacation as a period of rest from work or study!

In our family, vacations have meant vacating, leaving, departing from, our comfortable home with flush toilets, shower, washing machine, and dishwasher. They have meant stuffing our kids into a broken-down green station wagon in the middle of the night and traveling hours until we reached a spot where we could sleep in a leaky tent, haul water, wash by hand, cook on two little burners, and use pit toilets (if we were lucky).

Vacations for our family—by now we had three children—began when my sheepherder hubby decided he'd missed camping long enough. "It is time to teach you about the outdoors," he announced.

He arrived home from school one day carrying yards and yards of creamy white canvas.

"What's all that for?" I asked innocently.

"I'm going to make a tent."

"Do you know how?"

"Nothing to it," he replied. "You just cut a bit here and there and put the pieces together."

He rolled the canvas out on the back lawn, borrowed my best sewing shears, and set to work as the lambs watched. This project took a year.

I occasionally glanced at the tent's progress, but, because I had ominous feelings about its eventual use, I stayed indoors most of the time.

Finally Kermit announced, "Well, I'm finished. Come have a look."

"Uh, what do you do for a floor?" I asked, inspecting his invention. "Or a roof?"

"I left a hole in the top for air, and we'll tarp the ground before we pitch the tent."

He added, "By the way, I hear El Faro Beach in Mexico is a great place to camp. We'll go there next weekend."

Did I picture serene waves sloshing up on a white, sandy beach as I lay in the sun soaking in the sea air, little ones playing quietly by my side? I knew better. But I did have nightmares about the forthcoming adventure.

Kermit compiled endless lists of what we needed for the weekend experiment: food, lanterns, potty chair for Wendy and Bonnie, diapers for Bruce, bottled water, stove, beach

26

umbrella, broom, table, chairs. He forgot Wendy's night light.

The morning of our departure he called out, "Time for everyone to get up. We'll get an early start and cook a nice breakfast when we arrive at camp."

He added, speaking to me, "The kids will sleep all the way, and we'll have a very peaceful trip."

"What time is it?" I asked, rubbing my eyes.

"It's three o'clock. The trip takes five hours."

We left Brawley at 3:30. At 3:35 Wendy cried, "I'm hungry. Want to eat."

"Hush, . . . sleep," I growled.

"Whaaaaaa, whaaaaaaa." Bonnie and Bruce joined the chorus.

"OK, OK," I screamed. "Have a cracker and pass them around. Eat the whole box if you want to, but shut up!"

We arrived at El Faro. Kermit set up the tent as I stood by, feeling rather helpless. The children emptied the cardboard boxes in which I'd packed our food and clothing and made playhouses.

Kermit cooked. After we ate our pancakes and drank our orange juice, he said, "I have a great idea. We'll drive to Ensenada, find a fisherman, and get a lobster for our dinner."

I dug around in the sand and shook off the children's clothes, then dressed them. We piled in the car, and soon we arrived at the wharf in Ensenada. Kermit motioned to a man who had dark, narrow eyes and thick, black brows. The two gestured wildly at one another—we speak English only—about lobsters. Kermit said to me, "I think he is telling me that lobsters are not in season, but he keeps a supply at his house. So we'll take him there."

The man squished into the car, next to me. We drove miles and miles as I wondered, *What's gonna happen to us?*

Finally we reached the man's shack. He hopped from the car, motioning for us to remain seated. He came back in a moment, grinning, and holding an enormous live lobster whose claws waved in my direction.

Kermit paid him five dollars, and we drove back to camp. Then my husband asked, "Where's the dishpan?"

"You might try the sand, *dear.*"

"OK, OK. Relax. Enjoy yourself. Don't be so uptight."

Kermit found the shovel, dug up the pan, rinsed it out, filled it with bottled water, lit the Coleman stove, and began cooking. He emptied a can of tuna and used the can to melt butter.

We dined on "Catch of the Day" and sand.

Rain fell, night fell. "Mommy, Daddy," Wendy cried. "I'm scared. Want night light."

"Nothing to fear, darling," Kermit soothed. "We're right here. Crawl farther down in your

28

sleeping bag, and you won't get wet."

"Whaaaaaa, whaaaaaaa."

"Hush! Daddy will fix you a light. Where did you bury the can opener?"

Kermit found the flashlight and dug around in the wet sand for the opener. He emptied another can of tuna and put a candle in it. After he lit the candle he handed it to me. "Ev, you don't mind sitting up a little while and holding this light until Wendy falls asleep, do you? I'm bushed."

The next morning we packed up and left El Faro. As we approached Brawley five hours later, I prayed, "Thank you, Lord, for our little cowpoke town."

Overloaded

When we camp we haul a trailer
And we fill it to the top.
It holds our tent and cots and bags,
But there we do not stop.
An ice chest and two lanterns,
Pots and pans and then a broom . . .
Hubby takes a look at things,
Decides we still have room
To add a table and our bikes.
Yikes!

5
How to Get Adrenalin and Get It Fast

Before long, the camping bug bit Kermit again. The children were now six, five, and two. I felt ninety.

He planned an expedition to Lassen Park in Northern California. We took our usual haul (the neighbors politely asked Kermit, "Are you moving?") plus Kermit's sister-in-law, Helga, who is the adaptable, rugged, outdoorsy type, and fourteen frozen chuck steaks. (We'd bought half a cow a few months earlier, and the steaks were what was left of the creature. Kermit decided to put them to good use.)

I prayed for flexibility before we departed.

After our fifteen-hour drive to Lassen and the five hours setting up camp Kermit said, "You know, one of the main attractions here is climbing Lassen Peak. We'll get some rest now and talk about it tomorrow."

Early the next morning Helga suggested to me, "Why don't Kermit and I go ahead and make the hike? It's far too strenuous for you.

Besides, someone needs to stay in camp and watch the kids."

I felt my adrenalin supply increasing dramatically. Suddenly superenergized, I prayed for God's continued strength, for him to hold my tongue in cheek, and for a baby-sitter to become quickly available. He was faithful to answer all requests. A teenage girl from a neighboring campsite kept the kids.

Kermit, Helga, and I drove to the mountain's base, parked the car, and began our climb. My heart pounded wildly as I sprinted the five miles up the mountain, always certain I kept a few leaps in advance of Helga. My chest felt like lead, but I plodded on. When I reached the top of the peak I shouted the victory and ran the full way down again, grinning at Helga as I sailed by.

She didn't spend the two weeks smiling. Her major complaint during the trip became known when she said, "I think you're a lousy cook." This was because I used my administrative ability and assigned her the task of thinking up fourteen ways to prepare chuck steak in a high altitude. (She's known as a gourmet cook.)

Kermit misinterpreted my mountain-climbing zest as an endorsement for camping. For our eighth anniversary he presented me with a bright blue tent. A commercial model, it sported three rooms, a roof, and a floor. And it zipped up! He also promised, "From now on, dearest, I'll take you only to state parks with flush toilets and running water. And no more steaks from old cows."

I knew better. But I was learning to flex.

34

6
Thumbs Up

For years I've envied people who could grow houseplants. I've tried African violets, philodendrons, cactus. They all die shortly after coming to live in our home.

I was discussing my other-than-green thumb with my friend Vina. So she told me about "Mervin," her rubber plant.

"I bought him when he was just a tiny sprout," she shared. "I spent a lot of time singing to him, talking to him. He's grown into a beauty."

She confided that there was a time she thought Mervin was going to die. "We had gone on vacation and had left Mervin with friends. He ended up being shuffled around from one foster home to another all summer long," she lamented. "By September, he was a mess."

She said his leaves were yellow and scrawny. "Then I pruned him and started taking care of him again. He grew a new set of leaves and is prettier than ever."

She told me my whole problem was that I didn't treat my plants like human beings.

I zipped up to Safeway and came home with two little spiders, which I set in my bathroom. Turning over a new leaf, I sang to them every day and stroked them lovingly.

Scott overheard me once and asked, "Mom, are you OK?" I ignored him and continued to follow Vina's advice. Slowly, but surely, my spiders grew, and roots began sticking out of their containers.

Nevertheless, when Vina made one of her regular checks on my plants, she scolded me. Dipping her finger into the pots, she lamented, "Poor things. They're all dried out. No wonder they look so puny."

She transported my plants to the kitchen and put them under the faucet. A few drips and songs later, they were rejuvenated. "Hey, Evelyn," she shouted. "They're pregnant! Look at those roots. We've got to divide them up. I'll bet we'll have five babies."

Next thing I knew, we were in Vina's car, headed for the local nursery. We came home with several new containers and a bag of potting soil.

"Time for another lesson," Vina said to me as she carried everything out to the patio. "Get down on your hands and knees."

Soon, I was up to my elbows, slacks, blouse, and hair in potting soil. I mixed goop as Vina tenderly cut open the plastic con-

36

tainers housing the pregnant plants and lovingly transplanted them into new, larger quarters. She cooed at them the entire time.

"Now," she said firmly, "plants don't like their little feet too wet, so leave them alone for awhile. But stroke their little leaves and sing to them. Pretty soon you'll have a forest."

As Vina prepared to leave, she said, "Remember the secret. Tender, loving, care. Plants are God's creations, too."

7
Time Management for Harried Mothers (And Others)

I adore insomnia. I don't know why every-one makes such a big deal about it.

Mine began with Wendy, who loved night-life. She gave in at three-and-a-half and started sleeping through, but I found sleeplessness so delightful by then I kept on with the habit. I've had it for twenty-three years.

When the children were small, it was a total drag to take them with me to the grocery store. They climbed in and out of carts, ran the aisles, and chased one another while I tried to corral them and think at the same time.

Back then, our supermarket stayed open twenty-four hours a day, and it was safe to be outside at night. I learned I could do my weekly marketing in a jif if I waited until my insomnia came on, dressed, and sneaked out of the house solo. And I felt far more refreshed than when I'd try to shop during daylight hours.

Now that I have only one youngster at

home, I use my insomnia for reading, writing, sewing, or just basking in the delicious solitude. No one knocks at the door, and no one telephones during my insomnia.

Once, just for fun, I quizzed a few imsomniacs on their nocturnal activities. The results amazed me. Sherri scrubs her bathroom tile with a toothbrush; Frank weeds his carnations. The more conventional insomniacs read, watch television, or write poetry.

Aunt Evelyn, when questioned, fluffed her grey locks and admitted to many restless night hours.

"What do you do about them?" I asked.

"Well," she said, slowly sipping the tea she had fixed for us, "first I try milk toast. It's fatal if you get interested in something."

"And if the milk toast doesn't work?"

"I do ceramics, at least I did up until last year when my cataracts acted up." She excused herself to fetch a box from her closet.

She sat down again. "One year I planned all my Christmas ornaments in the night. They turned out to be my best," she mused as she opened the box and proudly showed me an assortment of miniature hand-painted trees, camels, deer, and Santas.

"Now that you have cataracts, how do you spend your sleepless nights?" I asked, admiring the miniatures.

"I plan trips. I'm figuring on going back to Alaska soon to visit my son and his family."

She added, "I also try out all the Bible verses I can remember, alphabetically—like *A* for 'Acknowledge Him in all thy ways' and *B* for the Beatitudes. The B's can consume all night if you're not fast."

That may be, because in her eighty-seven years, sixty of them as a minister's wife, Evelyn has learned plenty of Bible verses. She admits that X and Z stump her, however.

My aunt does confess to sneaking in a few catnaps here and there. "Good training if you want to be at your best during your imsomnia," she says. Hard for young mothers, though.

My theory is that if you can't sleep, why waste time in bed? Enjoy your insomnia—plan for it, relish it, delight in every moment. The time may come when you sleep through the night and can no longer derive productivity from those moonlight hours.

When that happens, you'll need to find time to read a book on time management.

8
The Kliewer Mold

Three of our offspring share the problem of dyslexia. That is, they learned to write everything upside down and backward, defying me to decipher their schoolwork in the mirror.

This startling discovery occurred when Bonnie began kindergarten. No matter how hard she tried, she could neither recognize nor print the letters of the alphabet correctly. During a parent-teacher conference, her instructor advised, "I suggest you have Bonnie tested." We did, and thus learned the official name for the unusual style of lettering.

From then on, every time another of our kids started school we visited the psychologist for testing. After Bruce's turn, the tester joked, "Well, you've got another one!" After Scott's exam he exclaimed, "Wow! This is phenomenal. What material for a data study!"

In addition to the dyslexia, all of the children were classified as hyperkinetic, and the activities in our home resembled a double-speed Charlie Chaplin movie. We never could find a baby-sitter willing to take a repeat assignment.

When the children were small, Kermit and I took several classes to learn how to rear our special bunch. We discovered:

1. The pros who teach parents how to deal with hyperkinetic children are usually childless.
2. The majority of how-to textbooks are written by the doctors who diagnose the kids, not by the mothers and fathers who live with them. (The parents are too exhausted to write.)

Everyone in our home interacts hyperactively with everyone else. This makes it difficult for us to feel God's peace.

I've often wondered why he chose me for the privilege of mothering this unusual family, but I do praise him for providing such good writing copy.

Several events have occurred during the years to ease the struggle, one being my mother Frances Durland's penchant for trips to Hawaii and her generosity in taking me along as chaperone. (Mother is also a Broadman author.) After all, these chicks in their eighties (mother, not me) need constant supervision.

Then Wendy moved out five years ago when she began college. She was happy for the excuse to leave home.

Last year, Bonnie took an apartment in a

42

nearby town. It's close enough to depend on us when she runs into problems. "I had to go to the hospital with an ear infection last night. Can you pay for it?" "I'm going on tour with my musical group; I need your large suitcase." Or, "I'm out of a job and out of food.") But she's far enough away to avoid us when she wishes to be independent.

Bruce recently left home, too, and visits us only once a month to enjoy a home-cooked meal.

That leaves only three of us battling it out at the Brawley Hilton, and the war has quieted down to occasional skirmishes. I never would have believed time could pass by so quickly, although I do use hair color to cover the gray hairs acquired over the years.

The truth is: When we run into problems and circumstances which challenge our sanity, God is right there with us and he sees us through.

Parents of hypers, hang in there. This, too, shall pass.

9
Am I a Mistake?

A few years ago Bruce and Scott got into a tiff. Scott, hysterical, came crying to me, "Bruce says I'm a mistake!"

I prayed, "Lord, give me wisdom and give it to me fast."

"That's not true," I told Scott, drying his eyes with a tissue and scooping him onto my lap. "You are quite a story. Let's talk about you."

Scott snuggled closer to me, and I wrapped my arms tightly around his little six-year-old form.

"God loves each of us, and we are all important to him," I said. "He especially loves making us happy. So one year when it was time for him to think about a birthday present for me, he decided to make it an extra-special gift, a birthday remembrance I would never, ever forget."

Scott listened intently.

"After God spent a long time thinking, he said to himself, *I know what will make Evelyn very happy*."

Scott grinned, pretending he hadn't the slightest idea what was coming next.

"God decided, *I'll make a little boy. Let's see . . . I'll give him blonde hair and brown eyes like his mommy's and a face exactly like his daddy's.*"

"Me?" Scott asked, giggling.

I hugged him tighter. "That's right, little one. God planned you as my extra-special birthday surprise. And you know what else?"

"What?"

"Just to be sure I wouldn't think God forgot me, he gave you to me a day early. That's why your birthday is September 4, and mine is September 5. And you know what else?

"What?"

"I love you."

"I love you, too!" Scott whispered, planting a kiss squarely on my lips as he scampered off to play.

10
Ever Get a D on Halloween?

Scott has always enjoyed costumes. One of his first included a ten-gallon felt hat which totally consumed his head. He wore it everywhere, even to the hospital prior to surgery when he was three. I suppose it was like a security blanket would be to any other child.

He often jumped on his rocking horse and played cowboy those first few years. Then he discovered Batman. When he was nursery school age, he flew around in a cape and horned hat.

Store-bought costumes for Halloween were never satisfactory to Scott, and he challenged my ingenuity every October.

Two years ago he announced, "I've decided to be a mummy for trick or treating. I need you to wrap me."

I replied, "Son, I'm not sure I know how to make you into a mummy, but I'll do my best."

"Matthew's mom knows. Just ask her. It's simple."

So I called Matthew's mother for instructions. She advised me to cut up strips from an old sheet, then wrap each finger and toe individually, tape them, then tackle other parts of the body.

As we cut strips together, I asked Scott, "How will you go to the bathroom?"

"Oh, I'll do that before we get to the final wrapping," he replied. "We'll save legs for last."

I began winding. After a couple of fingers, I found our system was not working.

"Lord," I prayed, "I can see you're sending a lesson in patience for me today. Thanks a lot."

"Can't you do it right?" Scott asked, tears welling in his eyes. "They keep coming off."

"I'm doing my best, Son," I said. "After all, I wasn't born in Egypt and haven't had much practice. I've already used up two $1.98 rolls of adhesive tape."

We tried again. "Scott," I yelled. "I'm sorry. You'll just have to get down your clown outfit and wear one of my wigs. It's getting late."

Scott made a few appropriate remarks in reply and ended up trick or treating as a very mad clown. And I ended up with a D in patience.

"What's that, Lord? You wish to speak to me?"

11
Our Little Computer

"Are you getting any money from your books this year?" Scott asked.

"I hope so, Son," I replied, thinking of our leaky roof and taxes, not to mention other unexpected expenses that always appear when our bank account is zilch. "What did you have in mind?"

"I was hoping you could lend me some money for roller skates and a bike."

"I'm sure we can work something out, Scott," I said, "but not now. Perhaps in a few weeks."

A wait of a few weeks was too long. Scott pulled out a piece of lined paper and a ruler from my desk drawer. He made three columns, heading them "roller skates," "bike," and "money."

Throughout the evening and the night, he figured out a way to finance his project, immediately. He took three baths during this time of intense concentration, the latest at 4 AM.

He came up with this: He'd raised a 4-H hog, "Petunia," and had sold her at the fair. With a portion of the profit, he had purchased a guitar, planning to become a famous guitarist.

A week after the purchase he announced, "Ralph plays the guitar real good, and he says my fingers are too little to play fast. He thinks I'd do better as a singer."

So our then ten-year-old sold his guitar and bought an amplifier. He rounded up a couple of friends and formed a group. With additional savings, he purchased a microphone and stand. The group lasted a month.

Now Scott had it all down in black and white. "I can sell my amplifier, mike, and stand—and buy roller skate parts from Brad. Then we can go to the sports store. If we buy shoes there, they'll put everything together for free."

My future businessman continued, "Then we'll have enough left, along with an advance on ten weeks of my allowance, to buy a bicycle."

I felt a bit hyper myself by the time he got through with all his calculations, but I did agree to take Scott to the sports store and talk things over with Tom, the proprietor.

Tom seemed to understand Scott far better than I and told him, "Man, you really got a good deal on these skate parts. Won't take me anytime to fix up a pair of roller skates for you."

Scott looked at me, then turned to Tom, and remarked, "I like reasoning with *men.*"

Eventually Scott also got the bicycle, which

was stolen two months later. So he finally traded his new skates to a friend who had an old bicycle. For the past several weeks, Scott has been back and forth to the sports store getting parts, paint, and inner tubes.

The other day he said, "I think I might trade back my bike for the roller skates. On the other hand, I could sell my skateboard. . . . "

50

12
Raindrops Keep Falling on My Head in the Shed

Kermit shook his head. "I can't believe this tax bill. More than two thousand dollars. How will we ever pay it?"

The bill was for a parcel of undeveloped property Kermit had purchased for eighty dollars an acre when he was in college. He'd always dreamed of retiring there, raising avocados and other fruit to supplement his retirement income.

Taxes on the Valley Center land, 125 miles west of Brawley, had been eighty-eight dollars a year for eons. But the area had recently become part of a municipal water district, and taxes had escalated overnight.

"I have no choice but to sell or to plant trees right away," Kermit reasoned. "I need a tax shelter."

Not foreseeing the new set of family problems which were to surface along with developing the property, I voiced no objections.

I had remembered the land from a visit there shortly after Kermit and I married. Dirt roads led through the twenty acres. A large pond, complete with frogs, ducks, and fish, graced the area. There were no neighbors, no telephones, no electricity, no running water, no bathrooms.

Kermit set our tent on top of a hill and announced that, hereafter, our family would spend weekends hoeing weeds, digging ditches, and gluing pipes together for a water system.

On the first weekend the tent blew down. Yellow jackets shared our meals cooked over a bonfire. Kermit shot eleven rattlesnakes, one of which Wendy found while toileting behind the haystacks. Coyotes serenaded us all night.

The girls and I tolerated the ranch, but the boys loved it because the weekends proved lucrative. Rabbits could be dissected and the feet sold for twenty-five cents each or three for a half dollar. Rattlesnake skins earned an even higher revenue.

My consuming desire was for Kermit to sell the property, using the profits to improve our Brawley home. Unfortunately, that was not at all what he had in mind.

At this point we came to a little impasse which remained unbroken for several years. The girls and I preferred to stay at the Brawley Hilton while our men spent more adventurous weekends at our Valley Center resort, which had now become the last resort for me.

52

Sometimes Kermit felt a little pressure, teaching all week and ranching Saturdays and Sundays. One evening he returned home smelling of dirt and glue.

Out of sheer desperation he shouted, "Other wives go with their husbands to dig ditches and lay pipes. All you do is sit around home reading and sleeping."

"If you wanted a ditchdigger for a wife," I retorted, "you married the wrong *lady.*"

Our brief communication about the ranch ended and so did our marriage, almost. Worried that Kermit might find a sturdier mate, I prayed about the matter.

"Lord, I'm not the outdoorsy type. Our marriage is straining at the seams. What's your advice?"

An inner voice urged, "Go to the ranch."

"That you talking, Lord?"

"Go!"

I prayed for another month, hoping God would change his mind. Finally I agreed to a trial run. One thing which I thought might be an improvement as far as facilities was the shed Kermit had built to replace the blown-down, homemade tent.

One night after Kermit settled down in his easy chair I announced, "Honey, I believe I'll go to the ranch with you this weekend."

His nose was buried in the newspaper, and it took a few moments for my statement to register. "Huh? What did you say?"

"I've decided to go to the ranch with you this weekend."

He jumped out of his reclining chair. "Hey, Bruce, Scott. Come here. Mom has decided to go with us this weekend. Let's go to Sears and buy her a Pak-a-Potti to celebrate."

"Yeah," Scott added. "That beats the bushes. And she can use my short hoe."

I spent the weekend on a chaise lounge listening to eight tapes, reading three books, and sleeping. I did note, however, that Kermit seemed to be in his glory as he tilled the soil. And I had to admit that the scenery was lovely. I didn't miss the television or telephone, only my running water and private bath.

I also noted that raindrops kept falling on my head as I slept in the shed. "What is this?" I asked Kermit as I shivered in my little blue bag.

"I put the roof on flat. I should have gabled it," he explained. "One of these days I'll redo it." (That was five years ago.)

Five years. Have I learned to camp happily? God has arranged some neat deals to help me feel content.

For example, he has provided me with a writers' group in the area and many new friends who like to come visit us at camp. And he has led our family to a marvelous church which we enjoy. It compensates for the snakes, coyotes, lizards, dirt, and bushes.

54

I felt proud of myself last Sunday. It had rained, and we had our own private river running through the midsection of the shed. I gracefully dressed for church in the dry section, then leaped over the water to the truck, and we were on our way. And I felt joyous through it all.

Paul teaches in Philippians 4:11: "I have learned in whatsoever state I am, therewith to be content" (satisfied to the point where I am not disturbed or disquieted).

Thank you, Jesus, that the secret of inner contentment is knowing you.

13
The Menagerie

As a kid, I loved visiting the zoo. Little did I realize that when I grew up and married, our family would have our own private collection of animals.

Our indoor menagerie began when Bruce started junior high school. He met a new friend who raised white rats.

Mark offered, "I have a good supply. Want some?"

Bruce came home enthused. "May I, please?" he asked, after explaining Mark's offer.

I pictured tiny white creatures with pink noses and beady pink eyes. Shudders of revulsion ran up and down my spine. "Absolutely not!"

"Please?" he pleaded. "Mark will even give me a cage."

"No."

Bruce thought, *I'll bet if I came home with just one cute, little furry thing, Mom will weaken and let me keep it.* So "Nosey" settled in with us.

One afternoon she disappeared. "Here, Nosey. Here, Nosey," we called frantically. When I noticed insulation strewn about my kitchen floor, I peeked behind the stove. There sat Nosey, shivering with fright.

"Bruce," I admonished. "You'd better keep Nosey in her cage. I don't care if she is bored."

Cage. Bruce saved his allowance and bought a traveling cage for Nosey. He had recently returned to school after being out for three years, due to a rare paralytic disease. We still made frequent trips to his specialist in San Diego. And every time we did, Nosey joined us in the car, the waiting room, and the doctor's office.

Next came "Pickles," a large male rat with a quivering pink nose and an appetite for drapes.

One afternoon I returned home following three hours of dental surgery. All I had in mind was Excedrin and bed. Bruce greeted me at the front door, scarcely able to contain himself.

"Guess what, Mom?" he said, grinning from ear to ear. "Nosey and Pickles got together, and they just had eleven babies." I tried to be kind.

Bruce found homes for ten rats and kept "Socrates," who loved crawling all over Scott in the middle of the night. (The boys shared a room.)

Bruce tried taking his rats to the ranch in

Nosey's traveling cage, but the lizards bothered them—and Bruce feared for the safety of his pets.

One morning he approached me. "Mom, since you are staying home this weekend, I have a favor to ask you. How about rat-sitting for me?"

What could a mother say to those pleading eyes? "Cage 'em up tight, Son."

When I entered the boy's room to feed the rats (I kept the door closed at all times so as not to look upon the debris) I found an empty cage, along with holey drapes. Hearing noises under the bed, I got down on my hands and knees to take a peek.

I found Pickles, Nosey, and Socrates. I also located the halves of three cookies, a set of weights, lost thongs, and a box of trick cards.

I crawled in further and grabbed. After a couple of hours, I had the rats back in their cages. Whew!

When Kermit and the boys returned I suggested, "Bruce, why not call your science teacher and see if the class would be interested in observing three rats as a project?"

Tears welled in Bruce's eyes the morning we drove to school with the menagerie. "My teacher is a lot nicer than you are!" he shouted at me as he departed, cage in hand.

Incidently, the junior-high science room is still decorated with lace drapes.

The Menagerie

14
Ozzie

"All I want for Christmas is a puppy," Scott announced late one November.

"And who will take care of him?" I asked.

"I will, of course. I'll keep him outside, and you won't have any extra work."

Kermit promised to repair our fence so that the animal could be kept safely out-of-doors.

On December 15, Kermit came home and took Bruce and me aside. "I have found *the* dog. He is Australian and Queens Sheep and will be perfect to take to the ranch."

Bruce inquired, "Does he have hair over both eyes? I hate that kind."

"No, he's sort of short-haired and spotted. His mother isn't too great looking, but maybe he'll be luckier. (Alas, as it turned out, he wasn't.) Why don't I take you to check him out?"

So Bruce and Kermit looked over the litter of pups, and Bruce granted approval to the one Kermit had chosen. When they got home,

Bruce divulged our secret to Scott. "Since I know about the dog, why don't we go get him?" Scott asked. "No point in waiting." I reminded him, "Your father hasn't fixed the fence yet. Where will we keep a dog?"

We agreed on the garage as a temporary residence, and on December 16 our family climbed into our gold Oldsmobile and drove to the country. We returned with a little bundle of multicolored fuzz which soon became monstrous and totally destroyed both my food allowance and my nerves.

The boys experimented with various names for fuzz, a mixture of brown, white, gold, and gray. "Spots"? "Wizard"? "Sam"?

"We've settled on 'Ozzie'," Scott finally announced. I contend to this day that "Torpedo" would have been more fitting.

Ozzie felt his quarters were far too confining, and I often left the garage door open to give him air. The problem was getting back into the house.

Ozzie quickly learned to wedge his way between my feet and the front door, shooting into the house like a torpedo before I could catch him. After a chase and a few leaps over the furniture, I would grab him and return him to the garage, firmly shutting the door.

Ozzie's quarters adjoined our family room, and each evening he howled until we allowed him to join us. He disliked the floor, preferring the couch which, in addition to being comfortable, proved chewable. One of his first meals was on the foam rubber arms of the sofa.

I had to relinquish cooking when Ozzie was indoors, because he would put his paws up on the stove and watch, drooling for whatever I was fixing.

A study on pets and personality development conducted at Yeshiva University in New York proves that when a pet is introduced into a family, interaction changes and becomes more complex. Not only does each member of the family interact with the animal in his own characteristic way, but family members interact with one another over the pet.

Truer words were never spoken. Pets can cause divorce—or homicide!

"Kermit," I exploded one evening after Ozzie had consumed the scrambled eggs I had fixed for myself, "I've had it with this mutt. You promised months ago to fix the fence. Here's the hammer."

So Kermit put a few patches on the broken-down fence and relegated Ozzie to the yard. Ozzie quickly learned how to get out. One of his first adventures was chasing a neighbor who was innocently riding her bicycle down the street; she screamed in terror all the way.

Ozzie loved the ranch, and there he learned to catch frogs in the pond and to chase rattlers and coyotes.

62

Nevertheless I must be honest and admit that when Ozzie met his demise I prayed, "Lord, thank you for giving us Ozzie. And thank you for taking him away. May he rest in peace."

15
Those Your Pigs in My Gutter?

My new neighbor knocked at the front door. "Those your pigs in my gutter?" she asked, smoothing her black pageboy.

"I'll have a look," I said. "I wonder how they got out?" I commented as I walked outside and noticed the pair of swine lolling in the gutter.

She pointed a long, narrow finger toward our wide-open gate and her newly squashed nasturtiums. I promised Kermit would replace the flowers.

I raced inside and called him at school. "The boys' pigs are loose. In fact, I imagine they're running down the street because that's what they were doing when I came in to phone you. I tried calling them, but they won't listen to me."

He said, "That's because you don't have any feed to lure them. Get a pan and offer it to them while you back up. Continue until you get through the gate. They will follow you right into their pen."

I grabbed the feed, raced down the street after the pigs, and shouted, "Here Petunia, here Charlie, here Sooie." My shoe fell off. I backtracked to put it on, but the neighbor's Dalmatian had already picked it up and had joined in the chase.

Faces appeared in doorways to view the commotion. Blessings upon the one who raises a variety of bright flowers, for just as the hogs stopped to munch, Kermit rounded the corner in his pickup truck to see how I was doing. He gathered up the pigs with ease and transported them back to their pens.

By now, I was a Christian, and the Lord had redeemed not only my soul but also my spirit of adventure and my sense of humor. Thus, when Kermit announced one Christmas vacation, "I need you to slop the hogs while the boys and I go to the ranch," I laughed and readily agreed. Little did I realize what a commitment I had made.

Kermit left precise instructions: "Two cans of pig feed, a can of meat scraps, and a little hay. Don't forget to check their water and do this twice a day."

Our normally sunny December weather changed abruptly when Kermit and the boys left the driveway, and it rained all week. I sloshed in the mud to the pens in our backyard, and when the pigs saw me coming, they lined up and climbed the fence, drooling for their fodder.

66

"Lord," I prayed. "How did I get myself into this marriage?"

I rose to the challenge, however, and organized my routine. I dressed in grubbies the first thing, waded to the pens, and fed the porcine critters. Then I stripped outside, came in for a shower, and dressed for work.

I repeated the ritual at 5 PM, only in reverse.

Aside from prayer, half the battle, maybe even three quarters, of being able to overcome dire circumstances is sharing our ordeals with friends. So I mentioned my escapades to Lorelei, not realizing her daughter also owned a pig and that my experiences were no match for what her family had gone through.

Lorelei's daughter, Stephanie, had fondly named her hog "Kermit," after her favorite agriculture teacher. Lorelei's husband had built a temporary cage for Kermit on the patio outside their back window. The pig was to remain there until he could be moved to more permanent quarters.

Kermit weighed thirty-five pounds and was in good fighting form. Squealing filled the air. "His eyes were red and narrowed to small slits of anger," Lorelei commented.

After caging Kermit, the family sat down to dinner at their pine table in the family room. They looked out the window onto the groomed and manicured backyard, the wooden deck and fire pit, and the swimming pool.

"Out of the corner of my eye," Lorelei said, "I saw Kermit race by."

She shouted, "Kermit has escaped!" Her husband and Stephanie put down their silverware, bolted through the door, and raced after the pig.

Kermit made a long pass through the flower beds and bushes encircling the yard. Then he leaped upon the decking surrounding the swimming pool, ran across the north end, up the wooden deck on the far side of the yard. He headed south, Stephanie in pursuit.

"Kermit raced to the edge of the pool and, without a moment's hesitation, did a beautiful dive into eight feet of water," Lorelei shared.

"Oh, no," Stephanie wailed. "He'll drown, and I don't have pig insurance." She jumped in after him.

Kermit did a credible breaststroke, beating Stephanie by half a pool length. He arrived at the shallow end, undaunted and squealing more loudly than ever.

After Kermit's capture he was moved to a more rural area, but his adventurous spirit did not diminish until county fair time.

We bid Kermit, Petunia, and Charlie farewell during the midwinter fair auction, which signaled their demise. For six months, my life was free of pigs.

Then my human Kermit brought in nineteen piglets for his fall students. Well, actually, the automobile association brought them in

when Kermit's flatbed broke down in the desert. "Most unusual towing job I've had in a long time," the AAA employee remarked.

Oh, oh, I hear squeals out back *right now.*

70

16
Shake 'Em Up

Bruce and I had just returned from an errand downtown. I had stepped into my bedroom to change from my suit into my blue jeans and a sweat shirt when I felt a rumble and heard the crash of our living room bookcase as it tumbled to the floor.

I grabbed my clothes and put them back on while standing in the doorway of the bedroom. Scott raced into the house shouting, "Earthquake!"

When the 6.5 tremor hit—the strongest quake in the United States for some time— Scott had been perched high in the new treehouse he had built in our backyard. He dived for the ground.

Bonnie, who had been resting in her room, made a hasty exit to a hall doorway just before her dresser fell over, face forward. Kermit ran from his desk to the safety of an archway. Wendy sat in her apartment two hundred miles away and missed the whole episode.

After the initial 4 PM quake ended that October afternoon, we rounded up the family. We joined hands and prayed, "Father, thank you that we are all safe. Help us to remain calm as we clean up the mess."

We assessed the damage. Every room in the house was in disarray. Books were strewed about. Plants, dirt, and broken pots mingled companionably on the bathroom floors. Bonnie's animal collection was in a shambles. Dishes had fallen from open kitchen cupboards. My china cup and saucer collection lay in pieces on the family room floor.

Scott's tree fort had remained intact.

We all pitched in to clean up. Kermit grabbed the vacuum and began in the family room; I swept the kitchen floor. The children picked up in their rooms and then the books.

Suddenly the aftershocks began. "Lord, I'm scared," I admitted. "Is this the end?"

The electricity went out early in the evening, and we gathered on the front lawn, joining other neighbors. One family organized a spontaneous, outdoor slumber party for anyone who was interested.

The children grabbed sleeping bags and flashlights and headed down the street. About fifteen others had brought out their camping gear when Ramsy, one of Bruce's friends, drove by, stopped, and threw his sleeping gear on the lawn. "Isn't this exciting?" he commented, grinning.

Kermit and I climbed in bed. Again I prayed, "Lord, my nerves are shot. Where is your peace?" Then the next jolt hit, throwing Kermit to the floor.

We also heard our crystal crashing in the pantry. Investigating with our remaining flashlight, we saw that it had mingled with catsup and applesauce. We grabbed other breakables and set them under the dining table. Cleaning up seemed fruitless.

"I'm getting out of here," Kermit announced. "Let's go sleep in the truck."

"With the straw and manure?" I asked. Kermit remembered he had brought home a load of sheep that afternoon and hadn't cleaned out the pickup. "The sheep!" he yelled. "What's become of them?"

He checked the backyard pen, and the sheep were all huddled safely together. "I'll sleep in the cab; you take the car," Kermit decided about our sleeping arrangements.

I grabbed a blanket and climbed in the backseat of my little Comet. Up and down and sideways it shook. Finally I decided to climb back into my own bed, pull the covers high over my head, and ride out the quake indoors.

Soon Bruce and Scott appeared. "We can't sleep down at Parks—too much commotion," Bruce explained. "I'm going back to bed."

"Yeah," Scott confirmed. "Who's afraid of a little earthquake?" I detected doubt in his voice, but big brother had apparently called little one chicken and Scott had to defend his manhood.

Kermit remained outside the rest of the night, and we found him snoring in the truck the next morning. The long siege had ended.

When we reassessed the damage, we discovered some of our priorities had been rearranged in the previous hours. The broken valuables didn't seem so important.

And let me assure you, every church in town was full the following Sunday morning.

74

17
Mothers Come in All Shapes and Sizes, and Some of Us Will Never Win Prizes

When Wendy was still in high school, she came home from a visit with a new friend and remarked, "You ought to meet Lisa's mother. She sure is slim."

"That's nice, dear," I replied, looking down at my cellulite. "God made mothers in all shapes and sizes."

I find it comforting to read Genesis, about how God made all sorts of things, including the heaven and earth and me, and I'm sure he uttered this very word, "Good!"

But is it? My shape has been an anathema to me ever since I can remember, rather like Paul's thorn in the flesh. I often ponder Paul's plight and wonder if he had a paunch. Perhaps his nickname might have been "Puffy Paul."

At any rate, over the years I've consumed more than my share of boiled eggs, lettuce leaves, and water hoping I would one day look like Lisa's mother. Then I learned that I am allergic to lettuce, so I had to try another approach.

I began jogging, pummeling my hips on the floor, and doing sit-ups. The latter program followed a visit from a new friend, an outspoken physical fitness expert. "Ev," she said, lowering herself to my family room floor and turning to rubber, "you must exercise. Let me give you a few suggestions as you join me down here." She added, "We'll have you looking sharp in no time."

She has a point, I thought. So I tried her scheme, but I still don't resemble Lisa's mother. I suppose it's because I'm me.

As I approach the half-century mark in life (already?!) I have come to some important conclusions!

1. Some mothers are naturally more endowed than others. Let's look at the positive side of that fact: There is more of us to love; we have good-sized laps for holding kids and fluffy arms for cuddling them; God loves us just the way we are.

2. Teenagers eventually outgrow the silly notion that all mothers must look like toothpicks.

3. Food is a necessity of life, and I like it.

4. The best I can do is surrender my appetite to God and ask him to direct my eating and exercise program, (not that I expected to burn calories chasing hogs and sheep all the time), follow his plan, then relax, and get on with living.

5. Pooh on Lisa's mother.

18
A Trauma a Day Turns Mother's Hair Gray

It was one of those exhausting days at work, and I came home totally fizzled. So, after putting on a load of wash, I lay down for a short nap.

Just as I dozed off, Scott burst into my bedroom. "Hurry, Mom, there's a flood."

I ran to the family room, and, sure enough, the carpeting was covered by an inch of water.

I turned off the washing machine and pulled out the vacuum, which converts to a wet mop. After I began sopping up the mess, I felt a shock and noticed sparks and water spurting out of the motor. Quickly, I unplugged the vacuum and finished the mopping up with bath towels and a fan. The machine had gone kerflooie.

As I reflected on the fact that I didn't feel up to coping with any further problems, Bruce raced through the door. "Mom, call the auto club right away. My truck broke down in the country, and I hitched a ride in. I need you to take me back." I moaned.

By evening, our carpet was semidry, Bruce's truck was back home, and I sat down to relax. "Lord," I prayed, "Thank you for getting me through this day."

I opened the newspaper and had read one story when the telephone rang. It was Kermit calling long distance from a conference he was attending.

"Hi, honey," he greeted. "How are things going?"

"Just great," I lied. And I added, "We miss you. You'll never know how much."

We chatted a bit, then Kermit announced, "I have some bad news. I ruptured my Achilles tendon playing tennis today, and I need you to come and bring me home."

Bruce and a friend volunteered to make the trip for me. The next morning while they were gone, Bonnie called. "Mom, guess what?"

"I can't imagine," I replied truthfully.

And she proceeded to tell me the following story. She had arranged to meet a friend, Gus, and attend a Bible study. He was to call for her in his truck. It was late and dark, so when Bonnie noticed a pickup driving around in the parking lot across from her new apartment, she assumed it was Gus.

She yelled for the truck to stop. Then she knocked at the window of the cab, and the driver opened the door for her. As Bonnie slid

78

into the passenger seat, the driver admonished, "Don't sit on that package!"

That voice sounds strange, Bonnie thought. She took a hard look at the driver with her big brown eyes—which got bigger when she realized the driver was not Gus. "You're not Gus!" she screamed and hurriedly jumped out of the truck, heart pounding wildly. Gus arrived a few minutes later, and the two proceeded to church.

Our traumas continued throughout that day and the next and the next—and included a $3,000 surgery on Kermit's ankle.

When I found time to catch my breath I prayed, "Thank you, Lord, that I am not a bored housewife and mother."

19
Pray for Me,
I Drive Highway 86

There's a slogan in our vicinity: "Pray for me, I drive Highway 86." That's because the two-lane highway out of Imperial Valley has been the scene of numerous fatalities.

The day I helped Bruce bring in our broken-down car, as the towee, I felt my demise was quickly approaching.

It all happened when Kermit, incapacitated due to the "Achilles' heel" operation, asked, "Who will go to the ranch to do the watering?"

Bruce and Scott volunteered, "If we can go to San Diego first and spend some time on the beach."

"That's fine," Kermit answered. "Take the Comet."

Bruce asked, "Are you sure it'll run?" The once-reliable car had recently been accordioned by a neighbor, and Kermit had had it stretched back into shape.

"We won't know until we give it a whirl," Kermit replied. And so the boys took off and had problems the entire trip, although once they had the thermostat removed in San Diego they felt they could make it the rest of the trip. They were wrong. As they came back into the Valley, the Comet collapsed and died.

The boys hitched a ride home and told me of their not-so-great luck. I was elected to take them back to the disabled vehicle and tow it in. Bruce, Scott, and I climbed into the cab of our flatbed truck and returned to the desert.

When we reached the Comet, Bruce tied it to the truck with what seemed to me a flimsy towrope. "All you need to do is sit in the Comet and steer," he instructed. "And hang on."

After I situated myself in the car, Bruce climbed into the flatbed and took off like a dragster. I challenge any one at Disneyland to come up with a more hairy ride. Never have I prayed so hard except during the 6.5 earthquake of '79.

"Oh, God, help me!" I pleaded as we sped around the curves. "Surely the rope will break at any moment, and I'll be thrown in the ditch." I kept slamming on the brakes to slow Bruce down.

In response, he turned around, waved his hands frantically, and scowled at me.

I never did find "the peace of God which passeth all understanding" until we pulled into our driveway. By the way, please pray for me, I drive Highway 86. There's no other way to get out of this place.

20
Cotton Pickin'
Sunflower Seeds

Sunflower seeds have been as much a part of Kermit's life as sheep. I find shells everywhere—on the car dashboard, on Kermit's desk, in pockets, on the carpet.

In fact, the shells are what drove me to nagging in our marriage. "It's bad enough for me to hop around sheep droppings outside," I thundered one evening, "but now you've taken over our family room. Every time I walk barefooted, I step on sunflower seed shells. Can't you be more considerate?"

Kermit, undaunted by my tirade, continued to eat unshelled sunflower seeds every day.

A marvelous feeling of well-being arose inside me the day we received a letter from friends on the coast whom we would soon be visiting. Ron wrote:

> Dear Kermit,
>
> We look forward to seeing you this weekend. We do ask one favor, however. Keep your cotton pickin' sunflower seeds home!

"See!" I said. "I'm not the only one who has deep feelings about your snacking habits." Kermit doubled up his seed consumption.

It's a good thing I can talk to Jesus about any subject, because if I couldn't our marriage would have disintegrated long ago. So I prayed about the shells after I realized Kermit would eat the seeds and leave the shells from here to eternity no matter how I felt about them. Solving the problem had gone beyond my resources.

"Lord," I confessed, "I hate sunflower seeds." I could feel the resentment surfacing as I let loose. "I've tried getting him to eat the shelled kind, but he misses the crunching. Our vacuum is too heavy to lug out every day. There has to be a solution, so please let me find it."

Nothing happened for a time, and I felt perhaps God didn't care about the seeds, although I felt better for having discussed the subject with him. Then our annual county fair came along. In one of the buildings where various firms display their wares, Kermit and I came across a booth exhibiting little light-weight carpet sweepers.

"Want to see how it works?" the salesman asked. Forthwith he dumped a package of sunflower seed shells on the booth's carpet, whisking them right back up with the little machine.

"We'll take one!" Kermit and I shouted simultaneously.

That was two years ago. The sweeper has replaced my nagging. Every night as he watches television, Kermit brings out his sunflower seeds and munches happily away. But I don't say a word. I let him eat in peace. Then when he is through, I hand him the sweeper.

God has an answer for every problem.

21
Rats on Hats

A speaker once said, "The Lord made a few perfect heads. The rest he covered with hair."

Kermit won't believe his head is perfect. Perhaps his self-consciousness dates back to the Christmas Wendy gave him a little hairless statue bearing the inscription, "Bald is Beautiful."

At any rate, he suddenly announced last summer, "I think I'll begin a hat collection."

I pictured stacks of hats—caps really—piled on his desk, on his file cabinets, on the television set, on the piano, in the kitchen, on my desk, and in the bedroom.

"And just where do you plan to keep them?" I asked.

"I'll build a rack for them and display them in the family room, dear," he assured me. "They'll look nice and neat."

He bought a rack of sorts where he tried to hang the caps. All the caps have adjustable plastic headbands and bills and don't lend themselves to staying in place. So we have caps on Kermit's desk, his file cabinets, in the kitchen, the den, *ad infinitum.*

Ad infinitum, I say, because as soon as the decision to collect caps was made, Kermit set forth on his mission. We made a lengthy trip last year, and we have a cap from every dot on the map to prove it. Let's see . . . we were in Catalina, at Echo Lake, ate at Bob's Roadside Inn, visited Portland and San Diego.

Then there are the companies around town who give complimentary caps to agriculture teachers. Kermit has them in yellow, green, blue, orange, white, brown, red, and multi-colors from tractor firms, produce companies, and feedlots.

But caps have a bright side, too. No longer do Kermit's mother, my mother, Wendy, Bonnie, Bruce, Scott, or I need to spend endless hours wondering what to buy him for Christmas, Father's Day, Valentine's Day, Easter, or his birthday.

Kermit is never hatless except while in the shower. He wears his hats to all meals, to watch television, to read, to teach, and to bed. The other night he climbed in wearing his shorts, T-shirt and cap. I believe it was the blue one which reads, "Beef Builds Beautiful Bodies."

Perhaps the Lord did make a few perfect heads. But the rest, he covers with caps.

86

22
Oh, That Tongue!

A friend, Marge, who works in the local Christian book store, asked a woman who came into the shop, "Are you new in town?"

The woman replied, "Why, yes, I am."

Marge chatted with her a bit, then inquired, "Do you mind my asking what church you attend?"

"Not at all," the woman answered. And she named the church.

"I hear they've changed pastors again," Marge commented. "How do you like the new minister?"

"Oh, I just love him," the woman replied. "He's my husband."

Marge tried to reprieve herself, without much success.

As Marge related this incident to me, laughing at herself, I thought, *I'm surprised that didn't happen to me.* My tongue has caused me more trouble than any other part of my body. I've found myself described perfectly in the Scriptures:

Proverbs 10:19: "Don't talk too much. You keep putting your foot in your mouth. Be sensible and turn off the flow!" (TLB).

Proverbs 18:21: "Those who love to talk will suffer the consequences. Men have died for saying the wrong thing!" (TLB).

James 3:5: "The tongue is a small thing, but what enormous damage it can do" (TLB).

Then I read, "No human being can tame the tongue" (Jas. 3:8, TLB), which I knew because I'd tried it for years. So I prayed, "Lord, I need you to tame my tongue. And hurry!"

I continued, "Help me say only things which are loving, uplifting, and soothing."

That noble goal has been tested to the utmost by sheep, pigs, sunflower seed shells, and children. I'd like to say I get an A on each examination. What I can tell you is that when I merit an F, the Holy Spirit gives me the test again. Sometimes I pass. Sometimes I need a repeat performance. I'm running about average at present, according to a recent survey I conducted. One of these days I hope to make it to the head of the class.

23
Huggy Bears and Kissy Poohs

My friend Sylvia was visiting an out-of-town church with her sister-in-law. After a few opening songs of worship, the minister announced, "Now it's time for Huggy Bears and Kissy Poohs."

It was the habit of the congregation to take a few moments to greet one another, hugs and kisses abounding.

Sylvia and Alice looked at one another. "I'll hug you," Sylvia whispered, "but that's it. I'm not kissy poohing anyone else."

Alice agreed, and so the two of them embraced briefly and watched as others in the congregation bear-hugged one another.

I understood how Sylvia and Alice felt because "greet all the brethren with an holy kiss" (1 Thess. 5:26) also proved difficult for me.

When I talked this over with my pastor, he explained, "That really was a cultural teaching, not a biblical injunction for today."

"Then why do we go around kissing strangers?" I queried.

He laughed, "That's a custom which has been with us for years. You'll adjust."

Alice, Sylvia, and I are not the only reserved persons who have trouble with kissy poohs. At a recent meeting I attended, the speaker told of his missionary years in a foreign country where the villagers, who bathe only once a week, are very demonstrative. Handshakes, no. Kisses, yes.

The missionary spoke to the villagers through an interpreter, preaching the word of God with all his heart. After the message, he stood to greet the brethren as they filed by. He found himself being kissed on the lips by seventy-five men, an uncomfortable experience, to say the least.

Then one husky villager gave our speaker a roaring smack, complete with a bear hug and tears. "My brother, my brother," he cried, moved deeply by the message of God's love. The speaker's heart melted, and he found himself returning the bear hug. After that, he grew to love the villagers and their customs. Huggy bears and kissy poohs weren't so hard after all.

I've observed that those hardest to hug— the men and women with halitosis, those with critical spirits, the ones who shake hands like fish—are those most needing the healing touch of genuine love. And I'm able to give that love when I'm so filled with the Holy

Spirit that I feel I'll burst if I don't share it with others.

My prayer is that God will keep me so full of Jesus that his love will flow through me to everything and everyone, even to the little lambs which come bleating at my back door, seeking affection.

24
Father's Day Special

"Dear Dad, This is very hard for people in our family to say to each other, but I love you very much and I'm proud to be your daughter. I know you've worked hard all your life to give me what I need, and I appreciate it."

As my friend Kathy wrote these words, she felt a tremendous release from the hatred and bitterness she had harbored against her alcoholic father for twenty-five years. She felt free and clean inside.

Kathy shared, "As far back as I can remember, Dad drank and gambled. When he would come home in a drunken rage, he would abuse me physically."

Then came the day that Kathy, as an adult, accepted Christ into her life. God began healing old wounds. One of those wounds was her relationship with her father. Kathy had been reading Ephesians 4:32: "Be kind to each other, tenderhearted, forgiving one another, just as God has forgiven you because you belong to Christ" (TLB).

Father's Day was approaching, and Kathy felt a nudging to write her father a letter rather than sending him a conventional card chosen at the local drugstore. As she wrote, so deep was her hatred, she cried out, "Jesus, I can't do it. You'll have to write through me."

Words began to flow onto the paper. After writing and sending the note, Kathy felt a tremendous surge of love for the one who had hurt her so much when she was a child, a new understanding of her father as a human being. The bitterness and resentment dissolved.

Kathy's father never mentioned the letter to her. But her mother told Kathy that he had cried when he read the note and had placed it in his billfold as a treasure to keep.

As I reflected on Kathy's experience, I naturally thought about my own relationship with my father, who was a good, moral man.

I realized he had never told me he loved me; he had never placed his arms around me; he had never seemed interested in me. As a child, I felt he rejected me. After I came to know Christ, I began to understand people in a new light. I learned that many of us have difficulty reaching out to others because of our own hurts. A feeling of intense love for my father enveloped me as the Holy Spirit gave me a new grasp on why my father found it hard to be demonstrative.

Following Kathy's example, I decided to

write my father. After penning a few lines I broke down and wept and wept and wept, until I felt no more tears could flow. When the purge ended, I wanted to fly. Then I continued writing.

I expressed my love for my father, my appreciation for his loyalty to our family and his material provisions. I explained the inner joy I had found through Jesus and the wish that he, too, would find this peace and happiness. I asked, "Please forgive me for any hurts I may have caused you. Have a special day."

A few weeks after I mailed the letter, Daddy fell ill and died. I never had a chance to see him, to speak with him. But somehow I picture him in heaven, free in Jesus, ready to greet me with a big hug when it's my time to leave this world for the next.

25
Farewell, Greyhound

"Take the bus and leave the driving to us." I thought Greyhound sported a pretty good motto. Especially after my first few driving lessons.

Because I was raised in the city, we relied on public transportation and legs for getting around. We did not own a car, so I had never learned to drive.

After our marriage, Kermit felt one of his new husbandly duties was to teach me. He pointed out a few fundamentals on our old green Ford. "This is the clutch; here's how you shift; there's the gas pedal . . . " Then he said, "The best way to learn is just do it."

We were living in Pacific Grove, near Carmel, while Kermit completed his army duties as chief gardener at Fort Ord. He took me out to Highway 1 for my first behind-the-wheel lesson. Mother was visiting at the time, so she rode in back.

As I darted in and out of traffic, Mother

prayed, "Lord, I'm ready. If this is my time, so be it."

Kermit, pleased with my progress, insisted I tackle the three-hour drive up the coast the next time we visited my girlhood home. As long as I was on the highway, everything seemed fine. It's when we arrived at Mother's steep driveway, with a city bus closing in fast behind, that I became nervous.

"Turn left, fast!" Kermit yelled.

"I'm scared," I cried, slamming on the brakes.

The bus narrowly missed my fender and came to a screeching halt. Passengers stared, and all of Mother's neighbors came to view the scenario. I switched to Greyhound right away.

After our move to Brawley I became active in an organization which required I travel a good deal. I logged several thousand miles with Greyhound one year, and the company loved me.

What got me back to driving was one of their midnight rides. I waited in a station for a 12:30 AM bus wondering, "Where is everyone?"

Soon the driver appeared. He brushed off his blue uniform and hopped aboard. "You're it!" he exclaimed, smiling and running his hand through his black curly hair.

I headed for the last seat on the bus. The

driver shouted, "Aw, come on. Sit up here with me so we can visit."

"No, thanks," I replied. "I'm tired. I'll just stay back here and leave the driving to you."

So we held a shouting match the entire trip. When we arrived in Brawley at 2 AM and I spotted Kermit waiting for me I yelled, "Oh, there's my husband!" I waved frantically. As soon as the driver brought the bus to a halt, I ran down the steps, right into Kermit's arms.

About this time, Bruce became ill and was hospitalized in San Diego, 140 miles west, for several months. At first, a friend took me to visit Bruce each week. Then I was needed for medical conferences during the week, meetings Kermit would be unable to attend. I had no choice but to drive to San Diego.

Driving to the store and to a nearby town for shopping were one thing, to San Diego over ice, snow, and mountain roads was quite another matter. I felt frantic.

I prayed, "Lord, you know I am petrified of freeways. I don't want to die now. My kids need me. What shall I do?"

A friend, a nondriver, offered to ride along with me for the first solo trip. If I scared her out of her wits she never let on, although I noticed she read her Bible during the whole trip over.

When I had to merge into heavy traffic, she suggested we pray. So we did. "Lord, show me how to get onto that highway."

It was as the parting of the Red Sea. After a few cars hurled by, the highway appeared barren for miles. I zipped onto the freeway, and immediately cars appeared once again.

Next I tackled Los Angeles. Before the initial trip I prayed, "Lord, I know you created angels as helpers, and I'd like about six today." In spite of rain, dark, and heavy traffic, we made it safely home.

By the time my Dad died five years ago, I felt comfortable with freeway traffic, and it was a good thing as Mother needed me to drive her to the funeral home, the lawyer's office, and the banks.

Furthermore, after I had been with her ten days she said, "Honey, I want you to have Dad's Comet. He would wish that." So instead of flying back home, I left the San Francisco Bay area in the little blue Comet one cold, winter morning. Fog swirled around that famous bridge as I crossed during morning rush hour. I felt a song in my heart and a surge of self-confidence as I drove the seven hundred miles to Brawley, marveling at the way God frees us from the fears in our lives.

Freedom from the fear of driving has brought me many blessings: new friends I'm able to visit; out-of-town writers' conferences; trips to visit Wendy, who lives two hundred miles away; a chauffeur's license from Scott.

In addition, I've been able to explore Hawaii on my visits there with Mother. We rent a car and take off all over the islands, even the hairpin curves on the road to Hana, Maui.

Whenever I see a Greyhound going by I muse, "There, but for the grace of God, go I."

26
Farewell Greyhound, Hello Mother

When Wendy, Bonnie, and Bruce left Brawley, I figured my chauffeuring days were about over.

I used to spend more time in the car than in the house. There were doctor and dental appointments, piano lessons, Cub Scout meetings, school activities, and shopping expeditions. With four children, all going in different directions simultaneously, I kept my car keys on a chain around my neck, ready for instant service. I'm finding life hasn't changed much.

Bruce enrolled in a Christian Life School program last fall and finished in the spring. He'd been cooperative about taking the bus home for visits. (I'd told him, "It was good enough for me.")

Then came the time he needed work to bridge the gap between finishing his Christian Life training and fall classes at the university. He was "without wheels," as the kids put it.

One evening he called home. "Mom," he

said cheerfully, "I have a lead for a job in a mortuary."

"Do you know what it involves?" I asked cautiously.

"Sure—fixing up corpses and stuff like that. I think I can handle it." He added, "And I'll get a free room."

He pleaded, "Mom, if you don't take me, I might have to move home for the summer."

"I'll be right there," I told him.

So he made arrangements for the interview, and I drove the 150 miles to his school to pick him up. When I arrived, he announced, "I have a couple of other interviews, too. And we need to go check out the mortuary college."

We took turns driving the 650 miles to various mortuaries throughout southern California. I felt certain I would end up in one of them when Bruce took his turn at the wheel.

But we made it safely back to the school, and I headed on home, sure I had a future mortician on my hands.

I'd felt stress about Bruce's use of his summer time. To be honest, life had become easier with the kids gone. My laundry pile had diminished considerably; my food bill, which was once phenomenal, could now be considered reasonable; and our household had become relatively quiet. The thought of Bruce moving back home was a threat to my security.

Now that we'd made the rounds of the mortuaries, I could relax. Bruce's plans seemed secure.

Our son, however, did some heavy thinking, perhaps about cadavers. Next thing I knew, he was on the phone again. (Long distance, collect, the usual). "Mom, I don't think God wants me to be a mortician after all. I believe I'll study psychology instead."

I'd just hung my car keys up when Wendy telephoned. She'd been studying in Portland and was looking forward to her spring recess. "Mom, I'm flying South to help a friend move North," she announced. "How about coming over to the coast to visit me? I won't see you again until Christmas."

Kermit and I decided that would be a nice family activity, but he found a conflict with school functions. So I was elected for the drive.

No sooner had I made those plans than Bruce phoned again. "Mom, I'm going to be in San Diego for the weekend. How about coming to get me, since I have a couple of days off?"

I took up my old job as chauffeur and put one thousand miles on the car, whizzing from one southern California city to another, then back to the desert.

I've often wondered what I would do if God hadn't delivered me from Greyhound or if we still owned Bessie, who could scarcely chug

102

around town, let alone cross the mountains.

But then I realized that God knows our needs and the needs of our families, and he is faithful. After the Comet died, the Lord replaced her with a new Toyota which gets thirty miles to the gallon (Bessie got ten). And he removed all fear of driving from my heart except when Bruce is at the wheel.

In short, I am free to be a mother.

27
Hula, Hula

A San Diego psychologist, conducting a seminar I covered for our local newspaper, remarked, "Stress reduces our ability to think clearly and brings about an imbalance in our bodies' nervous systems."

That explains everything, I thought. *No wonder I'm neurotic.*

He continued, "I feel anyone can learn to relax. Whatever works for you is fine. But it is important when you reach a deep feeling of relaxation to become aware of those inner feelings so they may be recalled."

So I prayed, "Lord, that sounds good. What do you have in mind for me in the way of relaxation?"

Next thing I knew, Mother was on the phone. "Honey," she announced, "I've inherited some money, and I want to enjoy it. How about going to Hawaii with me, just the two of us?"

"My suitcase is packed," I assured her.

Knowing that God had arranged for me to be away from Kermit, the children, Ozzie, pigs, and sheep for a week made it easy to forget them as the jet left the runway en route to Oahu.

I quickly learned to relax as I luxuriated in a quiet hotel, sunbathed on sunny beaches, and drove around viewing waterfalls and lush flower gardens. *Would I,* I pondered, *be able to recall these feelings upon my return to Brawley? Would I ever again be able to sleep in a bag in a shed?*

Doubt disappeared momentarily when I returned home invigorated, renewed, and refreshed. For a whole day I tackled traumas with ease—the paint Wendy had spilled on the carpet in the living room while I was away, the bank overdraft caused when I was not home to do the books, the week of collected dust and grime and dishes.

The second day I realized I'd better recapture the Hawaiian memories posthaste. I have a friend who has a large swimming pool nestled among palm trees. *With eyes closed,* I reasoned, *I could muse that I was on Waikiki.* So that's what I did until relaxation came again.

Mother had more of a problem with recall, what with the San Francisco fog. So she began the delightful custom of taking me on an annual trip with her to the islands. We'll leave again soon.

28
Speaking of Mother

My mother, Frances, is a 4'11" dynamo—a real, honest-to-goodness spring chicken.

The reason I know that is because last year we took a color course together. I'd already determined my season was spring, but I enrolled in the class because it included such vital subjects as "Dressing Thin."

Prior to the class, I'd bought yards and yards of fabric in spring colors and planned to sew up a new wardrobe for myself. I had lavenders, corals, light navy, peach—if the color was in the book, I'd found it.

Mother had come along to class as an observer since she was visiting me for a couple of weeks. She may be ninety chronologically, but it ends there. Her curiosity got the best of her, and soon she was in front of the class, checkbook in hand, ready to be color-draped.

Happily, she turned out to be a "Spring," the season of eternal youth. Alas, I ended up an "Autumn," and Mother ended up with my new wardrobe.

She claims she's the best-dressed senior citizen in her town. As a spring chicken, Mother likes new adventures, and she has had many over the years.

At one time, she had a flourishing writing career, which she relinquished to oil painting when arthritis set in. However, when I embarked on my own writing ministry, Mother decided to resume hers.

Although she vehemently denies harboring a spirit of competition, when I made my first sale Mother hobbled right up to the nearest stationery store and bought herself a soft-touch electric typewriter.

She didn't waste any time getting to work, either. She says, "I'll be dead by the time I hear from publishers if I don't hurry." So she whips them out fast, and so far has written three books.

One of her most exciting moments came when one publisher, Broadman, arranged for her book, *Growing in God's Love,* to be presented during a morning church service. Incidentally, the book was released on her eighty-eighth birthday.

She bought a blue dress for the occasion. Her minister gave a brief synopsis of the book, in glowing terms, then called Mother forward. Everyone in the congregation stood and applauded her as she received his kiss. She has it all on tape, and it brings her much joy to relive those glorious moments.

Recently, a television camera crew showed up on her doorstep and filmed a feature story on her for an inspirational program.

That's what Mother is—an inspiration. Her deep faith and love for others have been a testimony of God's Presence in her life.

Mother has her serious side, but she enjoys life to the hilt. Last year, for the first time in five decades, she slipped into a bathing suit during our Hawaiian sojourn and took a dip in the ocean, using her trusty brown cane for support.

Although she declined to enroll in the snorkeling class I took, she says things will be different this year now that I'm bringing along my own equipment. Mother vows she will don my mask and fins and try the sport herself.

And I'll bet she does.

29
Finding One's Niche

"Boy, times are tough," Kermit commented about four years ago. "It would sure help us out if you would work."

I retorted, "And just what do you think I do all day long?"

He replied, "I mean the kind of work that makes money, like an outside job."

I cringed. I often had nightmares about work because of several past fiascos, the latest a day-care center in our home. I also remembered a few college jobs which were not successful. The first had been in a cannery.

I had worked on an assembly line, standing in front of a conveyor belt. As apricot halves came down the conveyor, I was supposed to pick out the good ones and put them in a can. But by the time I made my selections, the fruit had whizzed by. My supervisor said, "Maybe you'd do better on wholes."

Whole apricots proved fine until the supervisor came to me one morning and announced, "We have located a pit in one of your cans. We are moving you to fruit cocktail."

At fruit cocktail, I stood at a turntable, along with several others, and placed a cherry in each jar as it came by. I enjoyed the opportunity of becoming acquainted with my co-workers, but the supervisor did not appreciate my friendliness. "It's peach pitting for you, young lady," she admonished.

After six weeks, both my nerves and hers were shot. I dreamed of fruit all night long, and she dreamed of firing me, which she did shortly thereafter.

"How will I earn money for college?" I cried in desperation. Then I found a job as a soda jerk at a twelve-stool drugstore fountain.

The first customer was a rather rotund woman who ordered a chocolate soda. My co-worker explained, "You push the water spigot forward for soft bubbles and backwards for fizz." So I put two squirts of chocolate syrup in the bottom of the soda glass, added some bubbles, ice cream, and fizz. Only I did not realize that when one fizzes on the ice cream, it splatters. The woman, who was sitting very close to the spigots, got a nice chocolate bath.

Next I observed that my co-worker made only one milkshake at a time. Rather than inquiring as to why, I assumed she was just inefficient, and I determined to use both rods on the machine simultaneously rather than wasting effort. I learned why my co-worker only made one shake at a time when I tried two, got a shock, and one shake spattered on the ceiling. The other showered the soda fountain patrons.

I thought about these and several other jobs when Kermit tried talking me into going to work. I said, "I'll think about it. Ask me again in a month."

I went to prayer: "Lord, you know I detest the idea of going to work. I want to be able to talk to my friends during the day, to read, to sleep. I have enough trauma in my life. But if you have a job for me, I'm willing. Throw it at me; make it clearly of you."

About a week later as I read a magazine which pays contributors to write stories about their problems, I realized I had plenty of material for such articles. I composed a voluminous list of our family traumas and set to work. I enrolled in a correspondence course on article writing, bought resource books, subscribed to writer's trade magazines. Within a few years, I sold a book.

In our cowpoke town selling a book is big news, so the local paper wrote a feature story about my achievement. The next day the editor called me. "How about coming to work part time? You can set your own hours."

I prayed, and the Lord said, "This is of me." So I went to work. I began with engagements, weddings, and obituaries. "If you ever have an idea for a feature story," my boss said, "try it out."

That night Scott came home from visiting a friend. "Mom, you should see Matthew's backyard. His mother has a million birds."

That sounded intriguing, so I investigated and learned she had forty-three, including a parrot who feeds himself peanut butter from a baby spoon. In addition, she and her sister had built all the aviaries and had taken a pottery class at the local junior college so they could make their own feeders. Matthew's mother's hobby proved excellent material for my first feature story.

Then I looked out my back window and realized the sheep provided further feature copy. So I wrote about them. And the more I wrote, the more I liked it. After all these years, I had found my niche—a job which did not prove disastrous. And I decided if one must work, it pays to ask Jesus what he has in mind.

30
Book Store Encounters of the Divine Kind

Prior to selling my first book, I accompanied Kermit on a trip to San Luis Obispo, California. As an aspiring writer, I had hoped to produce something saleable while my husband attended a conference, but nothing would jell.

Bored with writer's block, I decided to spend the afternoon downtown at Jan's Bible Book store.

It was a bright June day. I had seen a poster in Jan's window earlier in the week announcing an autograph party for a prominent author. I thought it would be exciting to meet a real, live, published writer. I eagerly took in the scenario: clusters of people surrounding a card table stacked high with the author's books; the author, dressed in a long, blue gown, madly autographing, toothpaste smile flashing. Also impressive was a suave, white-haired gentleman who was deep in conversation with Jan.

He must be an important publisher, I decided. I discreetly strained my ears to overhear their conversation, and I wished the man knew I was a potential writer.

After a couple of hours, I pulled myself away from my dreams and walked back to the motel. The next day my husband and I headed home, four hundred miles south.

Two years passed. I became more prolific and wrote a book which found its way to the West Coast acquisitions editor of an Eastern publishing house.

A couple of days after I mailed him the manuscript, my phone rang. Introducing himself, the acquisitions editor said, "I don't know why I read your book . . . I have a stack a mile high . . . but I like it. I'll be in touch."

A few days later, he called again. "I'm driving through your town on the way to Arizona. How about breakfast Thursday?"

We set up the appointment for a restaurant near my home.

I went to bed. Soon I was deep into a dream. A voice seemed to speak to me. "Evelyn," it said. "When you see him you will know him." I hazily pictured a suave, white-haired gentleman.

The next morning as I pulled up to the restaurant, I spotted him. He was dressed in gray slacks and a maroon sweater. After I parked the car, I got out and introduced myself. We went inside, took a booth, and ordered.

While we waited for our scrambled eggs, I

asked, "Did you happen to be in Jan's Bible Book Store in San Luis Obispo a couple of years ago? It was in June . . . the day . . . held an autograph party."

"Indeed I was," he replied. "I remember that day well. But how did you. . . . ?"

I explained. Then the editor talked some more about my book, how he was certain his firm would buy it, what they would do for promotion. "What are your future writing plans?" he inquired.

I mentioned a second book in progress.

Breakfast over, we parted and he promised to keep in touch. Although the firm did not buy that first manuscript (it floated around another couple of years before finding its home), I did write the second book. The acquisitions editor rushed it to his publisher, and they bought it immediately.

I felt fantastic about the whole affair—a book, by me. That is, until prepublication browsing revealed a dozen other books on the same subject. Anxiety took hold, and I wondered what kind of a push the publisher would give my work.

My tension dissolved during a second trip to San Luis Obispo in 1977. While there I met a woman who said, "I want you to meet a friend of mine. Her name is Jan, and she owns a book store in town. Perhaps we can have lunch together."

During lunch Jan eyed her watch nervously.

Finally she said, "I must get back to the store. I have a book salesman coming in this afternoon with his company's new fall catalog."

She mentioned the publishing firm involved, which happend to be *my* publisher.

I noted the fact, and Jan said, "Well, then, let's have some fun."

She hid me behind a partition. I strained to listen as the salesman, who makes it to Jan's for about fifteen minutes once a year, presented the new books. I wished all the while for more acute hearing.

After he gave his pitch on my new book, Jan told the salesman, "The author is here. Want to meet her?"

"She is, she is, where is she?" he stammered. "This has never happened to me before!"

I joyfully jumped out of hiding and pumped his hand, all the while praising God for his confirmation of my writing ministry.

116

31
Granny Goes Pac-Man

I have a bike the kids call "The Granny." It is blue and rusty, and I bought it for seven dollars more than twenty years ago. Granny has served me well.

Many times when I've been without a car, Granny has pedaled me to the store. And when my body has expanded and needs de-bulging, she's been right there, ready for service.

I've never had to worry about locking her up because she looks . . . well . . . decrepit.

But she works.

There was a time, not long ago, when I would ride Granny and my children refused to acknowledge me as their mother.

Last Christmas, my husband bought me a secondhand multispeed bike with hand brakes. I've almost lost my life on several occasions—trying to figure it all out as I sped through intersections and stop signs, my feet whizzing backwards as I tried to bring the thing to a halt. I long for Granny, with her

predictable footbrake and no speeds at all.
But Granny has been adopted by Scott.

Let me explain. Scott's own bicycles, in disrepair, rest upside down on the back patio. The desire to fix them is long gone. The roller skates hide under his bed; the skateboard sits in the garage, unused.

Pac-Man has come to town.

And Granny has proved her worth, for she transports Scott to and from the arcades with utmost reliability.

Pac-Man has become an obsession. There is the Pac-Man T-shirt, the Pac-Man cap, and the Pac-Man books explaining "How to Munch the Monsters."

"What's all that about?" I asked Scott one evening, as he studied various patterns in the book.

He tried to explain. "There are four monsters. They are red, light blue, orange or yellow, and pink. When you eat the energizers, the monsters turn blue and you eat them for points. The first one you eat is worth two hundred points; the second, four hundred; and so on. Get it?"

He continued, "All you can eat is four, and you either eat them or they eat you." (What I did understand is that if you don't eat them, they eat your weekly allowance in a hurry.)

In order to learn how to eat the monsters, Scott spends hours copying patterns and memorizing them. The Pac-Man book proclaims, "Impress and dazzle your friends."

Scott says, "I impress and dazzle by using three patterns. They are the doughnut dazzler, the suicide, and the ghost."

One of my regrets in reviewing my life as a mother is that I wasn't as good a listener as I feel mothers should be. I have been trying to reform, but struggling to absorb all this Pac-Man stuff has tested my patience to the utmost.

At any rate, I've learned that if Scott has three men left after an hour's play, he can sell them for twenty-five cents each, thus coming out ahead, saving his allowance for giant-sized Cokes.

He further explained, "Sometimes I play doubles—that is, with a partner. If my partner has to leave, I sell his share to someone else. It's a pretty good deal."

At the present time, Scott is Pac-Man champion of Brawley, an honor held in high esteem. Since he is the nonathletic type, I'm happy that God has allowed him this notable achievement.

How long the Pac-Man phase will last is debatable—probably not as long as it will take this book to get into print.

What lies ahead? Scott has decided to become a computer scientist. Can you imagine the conversations we will have then as he tries to explain life to me?

32
Northward Ho and Southward Baa

After Wendy finished four years of college in Southern California and worked for a year, she decided to head north to pursue graduate studies at Portland State University in Oregon. She was to be in the psychology department, perhaps a major subconsciously chosen because of her compelling desire to figure out our family—a formidable task.

In order to move her northward, we bought a small shell for our Toyota truck, then hitched up our little box trailer for her belongings. Kermit painted it bright yellow, his favorite color, for the event.

We felt rather sentimental about the trailer, as we had first used it when Kermit married me and moved me from Mother's to Monterey. And, of course, it had been used extensively over the years for sheep, this trip no exception.

We packed Wendy's possessions to overflowing, crammed her and Scott into the camper, and headed north, visiting various friends and relatives en route. Kermit also stopped several times to telephone other sheepherders.

When we arrived in Portland and began hunting for Wendy's apartment, Kermit ran a red light in his confusion. Horns blared and people shouted as he zipped through the intersection.

Circling around, he found himself back at the same spot. "What'd you do," Scott asked, "Come back to apologize?"

We finally located the apartment in an older section of town—so old, in fact, that the rings used in pioneer days to tie horses to the curb were still intact. Noting the address on the red brick building, 1515 S. W. Jefferson, Scott's eyes grew large. "Gee, Wendy, they sure built your place a long time ago!"

Indeed, the building looked as if parts of it were put together in the 1500s. Through various remodelings the place now boasted an old-fashioned white bathtub with claw feet, a bare light bulb hanging from the ceiling, a quaint little kitchen. At least it sported new rust-colored carpeting.

After settling Wendy in and walking to the university for a tour, then asking God to bless her and her studies, we headed southward again. En route, Kermit gazed dreamily at the lambs gracing the Oregon countryside. "We'll check them out next year," he determined. "Perhaps we can bring a few home."

Not that we came home empty-handed. In Northern California we picked up eight lambs and put them in the box trailer.

Each time we stopped for gas or a meal, the lambs drew comments and surprised looks. They provided great highway entertainment for tired, bored children, and we often noted cars pulling up behind us, grateful that we offered a respite for their kids.

We arrived home late one Friday evening, and the lambs were put to pasture on our lawn, since the mower was broken. The next day Kermit left for the ranch in Valley Center. I was left behind to sheep-sit.

Before Kermit departed I commented, "I hope you don't plan on my chasing sheep all over town. I trust you have checked the fence holes?" I sounded like a record, repeating our annual conversation.

The sheep mowed our lawn until Sunday. Just as I completed dressing for church, I heard a knock on our front door. "Did you know your sheep are running down the alley?" a young neighbor boy inquired.

We'd come full circle. I rounded up neighbors, who all pitched in to catch lambs. We all had a good morning constitutional. I even had presence of mind to grab my camera and snap a few candid shots of the event.

Then I went on to church.

122

33
Where Catastrophes Abound, So Does God

Before I gave my heart to Jesus, I thought of life as one continuous disaster. The daily traumas caused me to throw up my hands in despair.

One night long ago the sheep, pigs, rats, earthquakes, and children got to me. I flung myself across our king-size bed and sobbed, "Lord, I give up. I'm going nuts. Take over." That was the smartest move I've ever made. And I discovered right then that Jesus is personal and real, even in Brawley.

Our life remains full of catastrophes, but I share them all with our Lord. He gets the problems. I get the peace and joy.

As soon as I met the Lord, he opened my eyes to some of the more positive aspects of small-town living. *How many people are privileged to watch a youngster ride down the street on a bike, pulling a lamb behind on a lead rope?* I pondered. *How many housewives get their morning constitutional chasing hogs? How many women step out their*

123

back door into a sheepherder's camp?

One of my San Diego friends recently asked me about Brawley. I responded, "Come see for yourself. We have a Western parade and rodeo in November."

She took me up on it.

Joy and her family drove miles and miles across the desert and finally found our home. After a few brief amenities, we took off for the parade.

"This is fun," Joy commented as we watched the Shriner clowns, the floats, the marching bands, the horses mounted with thousands of dollars in silver. "We never get to see anything like this in the city."

I said, "But you get stores and the ocean. You can't have everything."

After the parade, we headed for the rodeo. None of our guests had ever been to one. We watched as cowboys competed for big purses in calf roping, bareback riding, steer wrestling, and other events.

That evening Joy and I took a walk. We sat down under a palm tree to watch a dazzling sunset. We shared how God can help us feel content no matter where we live.

As brilliant hues of gold, orange, and flaming pink lit the sky I said, "You know, Joy, I've decided cowpoke towns aren't so bad after all."

Epilogue

The events in this book, not always in sequence, might confuse you. (Our family confuses me, too.)

At present, and heaven only knows for how long, Bruce plans to be in a university two hundred miles from home. Wendy hopes to stay in Portland, more than one thousand miles north. Bonnie says she's staying close to home, and Scott has no choice but to live with us.

Kermit still shears sheep in our backyard, and often there are twenty-five tied up along the fence as fairtime approaches. He goes nearly every weekend to our avocado grove in Valley Center. I try to be a good sport, not complain about the leaky shed, and pick a little fruit. I prefer napping on my chaise, however.

Mother turned ninety this fall and says she's too old and her arthritis too rampant for her to write any more books. She also worries, as she has for the past five years, that her body will no longer survive a trip to Hawaii. I don't believe a word of it.

What hasn't changed is our love for Jesus, which grows deeper each day as we study his Word to us, pray, and fellowship with other Christians.

Without Jesus, I'd never survive this crazy life. Would you? I think our Lord makes living fun and exciting. And I hope you do, too.